DIRECTORS LEADERS TEAMS

INSIGHTS IN ORGANISATION MANAGEMENT

THE GOOD AND NOT SO GOOD SIDES OF ORGANISATIONS

RAJENDRA SINGH BOHORA

WORLD CLASS QUALITY AND SERVICE

COMPETITIVE COST AND REASONABLE PROFIT

PROGRESSIVE AND LONG TERM VISION

EFFECTIVE AND HONEST LEADERSHIP

TEAM WORK AND EQUAL OPPORTUNITY

CHALLENGING PLANS BUT REALISTIC

SUPPORT FOR TALENT AND DESIRE TO EXCEL

RESPECT FOR RULES AND REGULATIONS

OPEN TO NEW IDEAS AND SUGGETIONS

NO PLACE FOR FRAUDS, SCANDELS, SCAMS

NO PLACE FOR EGO, GROUPISM, CORRUPTION

TOP MANAGEMENT TO LEAD BY EXAMPLE

CONTROL TOP LEVEL, OTHERS WILL FOLLOW

A NOTE ON THE AUTHOR

The Author is a Mechanical Engineer and Management Professional, having wide experience in various fields like Manufacturing, Projects, Joint Venture with Multi National, Green Field Projects, Training, Administration, etc, and has come in contact with people at all Levels and Age Groups in Industry and Outside World. Has interest in writing on various subjects related to Industry, Institutions, Society, and different aspects of Life. Would like to share own thoughts, feelings, observations and experiences of the last 76 years of life, so that readers can look for possible areas of change or improvement, if any, at working place as well as in personal life.

Other interests include Poetry, Reading and Social Service.

Some of his Articles have been published in the Past. Two Hindi Poetry Books and a Book titled "Happy Meaningful Life", have also been published.

PREFACE

Due to wide difference in cultural practices, languages and prevailing environment from place to place all over the world, the perceptions, preferences, priorities and practices are bound to vary from one Country to another Country, one Region to another Region and even from one State to another State. All these have an impact on everyone's life, group behaviour and also on most of the Organisations.

Although a lot of good work is being done by most of the people, which is worth praising, due to which world is making fast progress all over, but it is also true that some of the well known Organisations have failed and hence there is a need to take prompt preventive action wherever required to avoid such failures. In the last few years, some of the Organisations at different places got adversely affected due to certain Wrong Practices or Greed of People in Power, affecting those Organisations severely, which is now well known to public in general.

ENRON (2001, USA), PARMALAT (ITALY, 2003), LEHMAN BROTHERS (2008, USA), SATYAM (2009, INDIA), and like that other examples are there of Frauds, Scams or Scandals at different places, which highlight what can happen to best of the best Organisations due to undesirable acts of People (especially Top Management Level), System Failures and Absence of necessary Checks and Balances.

These examples also highlight how people at various levels including highest level in the Organisation and Outside Agencies can fail or get mismanaged, and in the process cause considerable damage to the Organisation as well as to all other stake holders.

In absence of required information, it is difficult for anyone to say which Organisation may fail in future and hence only way to prevent such a situation by every Organisation is to carry out regular health check up of the Organisation and take suitable measures on a regular basis.

The infamous cases of Sterling Biotech, IL&FS, Yes Bank, DHFL, Nirav Modi, in India are now in public knowledge and like that cases keep on coming up in various Countries all over the World on a regular basis. Precision Castparts Corp., a Business Organisation in USA, ended up with a problem in hand when it took over some Business Units from a German Organisation in 2017, and later on found certain serious irregularities in old records which were confirmed through an Arbitration Award in USA in July, 2020. What finally happens in all such cases will vary from case to case basis.

The list of such infamous cases is long enough. Some more Organisations and Individuals keep on getting added to it, year after year. In all such cases, failure of Systems and Controls, Corporate Governance, Auditors, Rating Agencies, Bankers, Authorities, and Senior Management, fully or partly, has been the main cause of the problem. Fake invoices, inflated revenues and profits, diversion of funds through various dubious means, out of books transactions, phantom customers, managed records of inventories, generation of black money, fake assets, etc., are some of the methods used for such fraudulent activities. No single person can do it without support and involvement of some more people and other agencies.

Even when such wrong doings come in public knowledge, absence of quick resolution process and timely as well as exemplary punishment to people involved in such undesirable activities, long process of justice, etc., act as a support for this type of unwanted dubious activities. On top of that some such fraudsters manage to run away to another Country of their choice and then it becomes a long drawn process to bring involved people to justice due to laws and procedural formalities of those Countries or due to support managed by such people. Money power may also play negative role in all such cases.

Although larger economic Frauds can impact Organisations negatively at much faster rate and reach to point of no return, but smaller negative activities in pockets at various levels can also create serious problem, as effect of such activities keeps on adding and may end up in having negative impact of same order in due course of time. Inefficiencies in different forms, leakages from various places, favouritism, greed of some people, etc., finally add up over a period of time and affect the whole Organisation which may put question mark on viability of the Unit or Business Entity. Wastage of available time at work place, in offices and in production areas, is one of the common inefficient activity of people, extent of which depends upon the way Organisation operates and also on the type of Management Style, Professional, Non-Professional or Governmental type.

Different undesirable activities result in higher costs, delays, and may result in the Organisation becoming uncompetitive in due course of time. Hence it is not that only the larger Frauds create serious problems, but other undesirable things in various departments and by different people at various levels, can also make an Organisation sick. Nothing should be taken for granted as things can change, and behaviour of people can also change depending upon situation and opportunity. At the same time unnecessary controls shall be avoided. Vigilance is necessary but it should not be overdone. People should love to work and should not be under constant tension. Most of the people like to give their best and work in the interest of the Organisation. Problems are generally created by few people only and such people have to be dealt with appropriately.

As readers go through the Articles which are part of this collection, they may find some indications about root causes and possible solutions to some of the problems. Timely action and serious efforts by all concerned is requirement of the day. It may be late, but "Better be late than never".

R.S.BOHORA

Email:- rajendrabohora@gmail.com
Twitter:- @rajendrabohora
Also available on Linkedin
12th April 2021

HIGHLIGHTS

Every Organisation and group needs a Leader to lead the Team to achieve desired results

A Leader can take people in right or wrong direction

All value systems should start from Top, others will fall in line

Although everyone in the Organisation is important, some count more than others

If the Top Management itself gets involved in abuse of power, then Organisation is bound to suffer

If the Organisation cannot separate out weeds in time, one day there will be weeds all over.

Frauds, Scams or Scandals can take place in best of the best Organisations due to Greed of some people and Absence of proper Checks and

Balances. "Enron", "Lehman Brothers", "Satyam", are some of the examples

For Board Room Directors, only criteria should be Capability irrespective of their Gender

In-Dependent Directors and Auditing Agencies should work impartially and with sense of responsibility

There are three main categories of Management Styles which are practiced in different Organisations - Professional, Non-Professional and Governmental Type

Nonprofessional things do happen in Professional Organisations, mostly behind the curtains.

It is necessary to see what a person is doing himself.

Behaviour of people also depends upon the Organisation's Culture

It is the duty of Top Management to develop a Professional Work Culture and not to support undesirable activities.

To work under an Incompetent Boss acts as a punishment for a competent person

The storm of Globalization is gathering speed.

Respect for quality, understanding future trends, competitive costs and after sales service, are some important factors for World Class Organisation.

Goals shall be reviewed regularly as per change in situation and time.

Some people succeed more than others due to their foresight and timely decisions.

Personal ego and fixations come in the way of success.

Money can be made at faster rate by gambling and other dubious means also. It is a question of what is to be achieved.

Some people can cause more damage to the set up due to their presence.

Table of Contents

THE SILENT KILLERS......................18

BOARD ROOM POSITIONS................27

THE "IN"- "DEPENDENT" DIRECTOR...31

WORLD CLASS ORGANISATION.........46

INCOMPETENT BOSS.......................55

SUPER BOSS...................................67

ORGANISATION ENERGY..................77

THE MANAGEMENT STYLES.............83

TEAM WORKERS V/S LEADERS..........94

SELECTION FOR TOP POSTIONS.......103

THE SILENT KILLERS

Many Organisations grew with time and became Country or World famous due to their quality, reliability, specialisation, ethics, professionalism and volume of business. All such Organisations had at least one or more person behind this success who had clear vision, who were dedicated to the cause and always kept Organisation's interests ahead of them. They not only worked hard but also sacrificed their family life and gave their best to the Organisation. It was their vision, wisdom, dedication, organising capability and hard work which worked as necessary nutrients and oxygen to the sapling which grew into a big tree with fruits all over.

Many could take shelter under such trees and enjoy the fruits.

However, with time, many changes take place and the same happens to such Organisations. Market changes do affect, but those can be taken care of by individuals with vision. However, the change of people brings in new style of work, norms, standards, and value system. If they help in nurturing the set up, then further growth takes place. But if the new set of people become complacent and get used to enjoy the fruits without corresponding efforts and dedication, then the Organisation's growth gets affected. It becomes slow, or stagnant or may go downward. It may not be realised immediately but slow poison of selfishness at the cost of Organisation, and lack of wisdom, sincerity, hard work, etc., start spoiling the roots and branches of the Organisation. These factors result in having negative effect and Organisation's performances start declining. The rate of decline depends upon the extent and combination of such factors and people.

Top Level people are supposed to guide the destiny of so many people and everyone is supposed to provide helping hand to them. But if they become more interested in working for their personal interests, others will also do the same thing and then it becomes a chain reaction resulting in deterioration. Although work of all the people affects the overall performance, but the actions of few at the Top makes lot of difference. Most people follow the Leader and it is the Leader who sets the Culture and direction. If the Leader waivers, whole set up gets affected. A ship floats or sinks depends on the way it is steered by its Captain. Some people play key role resulting in success or failure of any task or achievement of any goal. The path of any Organisation remains full of uncertainties and obstacles. The judgment of people, who decide the policies, makes lot of difference. However, the success does not mean only profits because even a thief makes lot of money, but that is not the image one wants to have for the Organisation. The problem comes when the Top Level People have a mask of honesty, impartiality, fairness etc, but actually give more importance to their personal gains and start building up the set up to suit their own interests. They continue to look for something benefiting themselves and hence the decision-making process gets coloured. Some people get around them to say "yes" for all their actions — right or wrong, and also help them by making it easy to make money or take advantage, wherever possible.

In the process, performance becomes less important. A blind eye may be turned towards poor or average results or the

Organisation's real performance may be kept hidden by manipulations. In absence of a proper forum for exposing such activities and as it is generally done by well-placed people, it becomes difficult for lower down people to take up and fight against such activities. They may neither have means nor capacity to do so.

All the pillars who built the Organisation get replaced one or the other day and new pillars take their positions. But these new pillars may not be strong enough or might have been discarded somewhere. Depending on their strength or weaknesses, more pillars may get added to sustain the Organisation and the process may go on till one day the pillars start collapsing due to their weaknesses, resulting in collapse of the Organisation. It happens suddenly or slowly depends upon the situation. Hence, it is important that everyone looks at oneself, particularly those who are at Top, introspect to analyse the weaknesses in themselves and come out clean. They must get rid of greed and avoid favouritism, shortcuts, temporary pleasures at the cost of Organisation. They must remain in position due to their own capabilities, support good performers and should be able to retain them. They should have no place for dishonesty and should remain away from anything which affects the Organisation adversely.

It is difficult to visualise the after effects of all the actions and hence the least a person can do is to avoid any personal gains or favours to anybody while taking organisational decisions. This itself will go a long way in building up a healthy, energetic, vibrant, creative, progressive and profitable Organisation and will provide a fertile ground for honest and capable people to work for that Organisation. This will also provide healthy atmosphere for good, creative work and will not allow the undesirable activities to grow. People will support each other and activities will become more productive resulting in an all-round improvement. Individuals will grow, enjoy the workplace, and the Organisation will also flourish by achieving greater heights day by day.

The Top Level should always remain light so that subordinates do not get pressed down due to heavy weight at the top and the Organisation does not crumble down. The base should be broad and strong enough and should not get spoiled or get affected due to the sickness of inefficiency or incompetency at Top Level. Climbing up the ladder should not be due to push or pull of others but should be only due to the energy level and capability of individual.

After reaching at the Top Level, the Person shall not go on

holding the position just because he or she is there and has support of few influential active supporters, but should be able to sustain growth and achieve desired results for all stakeholders without finding out excuses and blaming environment. If necessary, the Top Person should be magnanimous enough to quit or move and make room for others who can achieve better results. It is very difficult for people to accept failure but only acceptance is not good enough for the Organisation. They should bring in necessary changes or get changed. Also, the actions should not be an eyewash, and changes should not be made for the sake of change, just to give a perception to people that something is being done. All new actions should finally result in improvement and better performance in a real term on a continuous basis. Hence, it is not enough to have only honest, benevolent, straightforward people at Top and to have a clean working atmosphere with nice place to work. It is also not enough to treat everybody nicely and have good working relationships at all levels but what is important is with all these good things, there has to be proper mission and vision and that should get supported by actual meaningful result-oriented actions. Merely dreaming does not help. Goals should be practical, implementable, cost effective and useful for Organisation's growth.

The Top Leaders make lot of difference — positive or negative and it is their responsibility as well as duty to remain in power only if they are able to build a healthy, vibrant, creative, progressive and fair Organisation on long term basis. Otherwise, they may be the cause of the downfall and may act as Silent Killers of the Organisation.

BOARD ROOM POSITIONS

Gender wise representation

Gender wise percentage representation in Board Room Positions in various Organisations is being noticed now a days, comparing its country wise data, and comments are being made that Gender wise these should be more balanced. Instead of discussing about filling up the positions on the basis of merits only, and availability of such personalities, stress is being given on percentage of Men and Women in such positions. Such discussions are more like filling up posts by forced reservation at various places even at the cost of sacrificing capabilities. Such practices may go on in public funded set ups where political considerations come into picture instead of required progress but it may be harmful for individual Organisation which has to manage and survive on its own performance.

One sometimes wonders why move is in this direction where performance may take back seat and other criteria become more important. Some people think that existing Gender wise representation is not proper because of Male Predominance and suppression of Female. It is a debatable point and actually needs to be examined to find out whether there are some capable Women who have been purposely kept behind.

USA could not select any Woman in the last two centuries as President of the Country while as India had Woman Prime Minister as well as President and so is the case with many other Countries including Bangladesh, Pakistan,

Germany, and UK. Is it a sign of backwardness and Male Predominance in USA? The answer will be definitely 'No'.

Board Room Positions should not be for namesake but should be occupied by capable people who contribute positively with sense of responsibility. There are reasons to believe that such positions in some cases are filled up due to other considerations, their connections or influence, rather than capabilities required for those positions. Such practices are undesirable and actually require correction as well as control. More discussion is required in this direction rather than Percentage of Gender Representation.

There should NOT be any minimum or maximum limit Gender Wise on Board Room Positions and should be filled up keeping in mind the overall interest of all stake holders and the Organisation's future. At the same time, no one should be kept behind because of his or her Gender and it can be up to Hundred Percent by any Gender, depending upon capability, suitability, availability and their willingness to really work in the interest of the Organisation.

THE "IN"- "DEPENDENT" DIRECTOR

This Article was first published by me in the year 2011 and is being included here as the content remains fully relevant in present time. As was pointed out, in absence of suitable steps, after "Satyam", more and more Frauds or Scams or Scandals, like Yes Bank, DHFL, Sterling Biotech, and others, have come out in the last few years. The role of Independent Directors is becoming more important and needs to be strengthened. It's not only for Indian set up, but is applicable for Organisations anywhere in any Country.

In order to improve governance and keep better check on performance of an Organization, it was thought necessary to make it mandatory in India to appoint some external experienced, capable and impartial individuals on the Board of Directors and call them **INDEPENDENT DIRECTORS**. The idea was that such people will not only bring in their expertise but will also be able to look at things impartially without getting influenced by the Whole Time Directors and day to day operations of the Organization. It was really a good idea. As it became mandatory, number of Independent Directors were appointed in many Organizations. These Independent Directors were supposed to not only give their valuable suggestions from time to time to improve the performance of the Organization but were also supposed to raise timely alarm on any mismanagement by operating people and try to prevent any possible damage to the health of the Organization. It was necessary to implement this idea properly with honesty in order to get desired improvement and results. Induction of these new personalities and honest sincere contribution by them would have definitely made a significant difference to the overall progress, subject to the existing culture of the Organization. Although it's not possible to make specific comment about the positive or negative contribution made by an individual as an Independent Director in a particular Organization, but we need to analyze the overall impact and impressions created so far. Good work done by few individuals must be praised but what really happened in many cases was bad implementation of a good idea. Many of the so-called Independent Directors were "IN" but remained "DEPENDENT", and did not serve the purpose for which they were really required. Number of them actually did not take these assignments with required seriousness, but enjoyed the status, fringe benefits and in the process also attended few meetings, made certain observations and then forgot about necessary follow up. The whole process of their appointment was faulty as it was not done with honesty for the purpose and their appointments were at the mercy of the people who were used to functioning without such external forces for so many years.

Some Organizations were more sincere and really inducted few eminent personalities as well as some experts in the field to get benefited from their experience and timely advice. Except in few cases where the benefits really might have come, contribution of such people also remained limited as their involvement was mostly through attending few Board Meetings in a year. These well-known personalities ended up joining many Company Boards and hence remained over busy. It became more of a business for them and a source of increasing their own contacts.

Directors were also appointed from Financial Institutions and Government of India or State Governments side, depending upon the shareholding pattern and investment made by them in a particular Organization. This has been a regular process for so many years and will continue in the future also. These appointments are made primarily to safeguard the interests of the Institutions and hence their approach has to be different. In any case individuals are appointed because they are holding a particular position in their Institution and hence, they keep on changing from time to time. They are not dependent on particular Organization for their induction in the Board and they are actually given these additional responsibilities for some time. Their focus is different and hence their interest remains limited. The Government owned Organizations have political interference and the whole approach of Directors is influenced by various external factors.

All this resulted in having additional Directors on the Company Boards with certain purpose and costs, but the purpose got lost as number of the Independent Directors did not contribute effectively, and the acting Directors were also not much interested in getting disturbed. Some of the Independent Directors might have made some feeble noises on certain issues in a meeting on a particular day and then forgotten about it. They had no intention and interest in perusing the cause. It remained limited to record their presence and show their involvement. The attendance in a Board Meetings could also be recorded by mutual understanding and consent taken on some issues without personally remaining present. Some of the Independent Directors remain more interested in taking advantage of the Company facilities for personal use including for their friends and relatives and even getting certain payments made by the Company for which they are otherwise not entitled. The operating people entertain such requests so as to keep the "Independent Director" in good humour, to avoid any uncomfortable situation or hurdle and to obtain a free hand for them. However, if any Organization comes in public eye for any unlawful activities or fraud, first among those who will try to escape from any responsibility and try to leave will be the Independent Directors and hence they are friends for good time only.

Then there are Independent Directors appointed by certain family-owned Organizations just to complete the formalities of certain applicable rules or regulations. These may be more or less paper entries. The fact is that laid down norms and controls are not as effective as required and there is negligible accountability of Independent Directors. Hence it is not serving the purpose except at some places to some extent. On the whole it is an opportunity lost case for most of the Organizations. Sometimes some individuals get appointed as Independent Directors for their connections, contacts, etc. It becomes easy to approach right people through them to get necessary confidential information, get certain favors as well as make settlements smoothly, wherever required.

The Satyam fraud is just one case which tells many stories as to how various systems and people in position can be managed or maneuvered and how one can be silenced by certain individuals for personal gains. It tells us how easy it is to fudge the Accounts or Balance Sheets and get these audited as well as certified for years together. It also conveys as to what extent people can work against the interest of the Organization knowingly or unknowingly. It's a typical case which conveys what can happen to the Organization as well as thousands of employees and how it can affect the community due to greed of few individuals. Satyam is a typical case conveying how one can manage to hide and carry on with the fraud for years together, that too at multi-locations without authorities or public knowing about it (or keeping mum knowingly) and that the whole fraud will get highlighted only when the culprit himself comes forward due to probably God's wish. It also conveys that not only the Directors but how the reputed Auditing Firms can function and how they can be managed. Unfortunately, the selection of Auditing Firms remains dependent on such people only and hence it affects their independence. Ironically the name Satyam means Truth, but what happened there at highest level was just the opposite. Like Satyam, there may be many more cases still unknown and the greed of few people supported by lack of proper controls will continue to provide flourishing ground for such activities.

In our country the politicians and bureaucrats have considerable public exposure and hence their images have been formed in public eye and the public knows how they function and what one can expect from them. Good and bad people in these fields are generally known but that is not true about the directors of most of the Organizations and about the so-called Independent Directors. Public in general has very little knowledge of their misdeeds and hence they are able to continue doing so without having any effect on them. "You take care of me and I will take care of you" works at number of places. One should understand that the Directors who are on regular role of Organizations also depend to some extent for their positions or functioning and benefits on topmost person in the Organization and hence they may remain silent observer or become part of the misdeeds just to safeguard their own positions or benefits or future. Some don't even come to know as to what is going on behind their back. This was one of the reasons for introducing Independent Directors so that at least these outsiders can voice their dissent and object to something which is not good for the Organization. But in reality, it has hardly served that purpose. In any case a person attending just few meetings for few hours in a year and only going through few prepared reports can contribute to a very limited extent. Such people are also careful not to become unwanted persons in any Organization in order to avoid a situation where other Organizations also do not like them. Even the present

Organization may try to get rid of them at the earliest. Hence the very nature of such a system is to compromise and make necessary adjustments. What is necessary is that the topmost person of an Organization carries full responsibility to build and maintain a forward looking, progressive, efficient and honest set up. The top person should not misuse his or her position and should not try to make rules to get benefits undeservingly and disproportionately. The top person should not find all possible loopholes to get maximum benefits for himself or herself. Misuse of power can be seen openly in many Organizations. Few top people try to accumulate lot of wealth at the cost of their Organization. In order to achieve their personal goals, in some cases, they also make systems or rules so that part of the booty goes in the hands of second and third rank people also so as to avoid any noises. What goes unofficially is a different story and is known only to few in the setup who become party to such acts just to retain their own jobs and also to get undue advantages for themselves. Lot of money gets siphoned off unofficially by few people in power and they use all sort of tactics for the same. Unfortunately, the shareholding community in India is not so well organized and the public hardly has any control on activities of the top management.

Question may be asked whether we require Independent Directors at all. The past experience and present state of affairs tells us that it has become necessary to keep them. The need is to select right people, make them more effective and provide them right atmosphere to express free and franc opinions. To make it possible, the Managing Director or Chairman or CEO or Head of an Organization can play a vital role and make a lot of difference. If they really want, they can extract maximum benefits for the Organization from Independent Directors by selecting only deserving people, really using their experience, capabilities and making arrangements so that their role becomes more effective. It's true that any Organization works properly on team-work but it's also true that every team requires a leader. If the leaders at top support efficient capable people and allow healthy criticism, the Organization becomes progressive, profitable, reputed and growth oriented. Then people can enjoy doing their job and contribute positively for all round growth of the Organization. Government of India, State Governments, SEBI, and Corporate Bodies have to work together sincerely to make an Independent Director more effective. At the same time individuals, who are appointed as Independent Directors, need to introspect, should not become greedy, and should work honestly for the purpose for which they are appointed.

WORLD CLASS ORGANISATION

With increasing competitive world and globalisation, it has become important and necessary for many Organisations to achieve World Class level in order to survive and progress further. Quality of products will always remain main consideration for competing on World Level. Unique features of the product, competitive cost, timely delivery, after sales service, etc., also play vital role in the competition. Adaptability to change and constantly improving to keep pace with the latest and future developments will also be equally important.

With advancement of Information Technology and increase in Industrial as well as Financial activities, business opportunities have increased manifold. Underdeveloped Countries today have access to the latest technology through Joint Ventures. Developed countries are interested in Developing Countries like India. But demand for quality and stiff competition has put lot of pressure on local Organisations. The days of monopoly have gone in most areas and Organisations can no longer afford to carry on business in the old fashion. Businessmen will have to see the writing on the wall and understand that there is no other alternative to competition.

The first thing is to understand own strengths and weaknesses. Benchmarking with respect to other Organisations and competitors is necessary. Unless and until every department and people involved are competitive and try to do their best, the Organisation cannot compete effectively. Merely talking about productivity related to the shop performance and output of workmen cannot help.

Organisations cannot become World Class and compete globally unless everyone believes in 'work is worship' and avoid all wasteful practices. What needs to be understood is that it is not only the technological superiority which is keeping Advanced Countries in forefront, but also due to the Country People, their style of working, respect for quality and their belief in dignity of labour.

Some wasteful practices, rules or regulations and lack of required facilities within and outside the Organisation may come in the way which may not allow people to concentrate fully on improvements and partly keep them busy on fire-fighting. To compete globally, all the agencies involved in the process, including Decision Makers and Authorities, have to contribute positively. Simultaneously, Organisations have to take effective steps within their own set up also to achieve world standards.

Anyone who has visited Organisations in the Developed Countries, or has tried to understand how those Organisations function, must have realised that they work with limited staff and workers, thus their production costs remain competitive. In Developing Countries including India, in number of Organisations, staff in supporting functions or indirect services are generally much more. Some Organisations on an average have more employees in various departments like stores, administration, marketing, purchase accounts, inspection, etc., as compared to Developed Countries who generally keep very limited staff for such departments. Also, in departments like personnel, labour, travel, medical, welfare, liaison, etc., they normally keep very limited staff. In Less Developed Countries and Country like India, in some cases, the total number of people employed in an Organisation as secretaries, clerks, peons, travel coordinators, mail room / pantry / canteen / guest house attendants, security guards, gardeners, and in other miscellaneous indirect services may be equal or more than the total number of people working in Organisation of similar type in Developed Countries.

Some executives may not like to reduce staff in certain areas, as it may affect their own comfort level. People try to build up facilities to get extra comfort, even at the cost of Organisation and the departments keep on growing unnecessarily. This results in longer chain of communication and more levels of working. Paper work keeps on increasing due to more people and efficiency reduces. In such cases, every office table takes its own time to pass files, decisions or for taking necessary actions. Systems get made to have checks and counter checks, someone to remind for the job and someone to file or move papers. The staff cannot be minimised by one department in isolation, if others do not follow, and hence such move has to be implemented all over to gain acceptability. Many offices remain devoid of latest equipment and gadgets. The ones who have may not use these effectively.

Organisations have to develop global culture to become world class and for that latest Information Technology, office equipment and systems must be in place. It is possible to improve office productivity in short period, if taken up seriously. What needs to be done is benchmarking the office activities and decide to implement possible improvements which can give advantage in competing with others.

For a better Organisation, everyone needs to take the first step individually instead of waiting for others to make the move. The same goes true for various departments and individual Organisation. A chain process has to start to reach critical stage and only then required productivity levels can be achieved. Some Organisations with less productivity may survive for some time due to certain advantages they might be commanding in a protected market, but it cannot last longer and definitely not when it is a global competition.

To become World Class, the Organisation should also take necessary steps to fight inefficiencies or undesirable practices, if any, in any form within the Organisation, like in selecting and placement of people, promotions, increments, purchases, material accounting, taxation, fund management, invoicing, customs clearances, imports-exports, travels, payments for public services or facilities and licenses. Organisations cannot complain about corruption in public life, government offices and politics, unless they themselves remain honest in their dealings. Some undesirable activities in some of the Organisations in fact end up in providing support to corruption in public life.

There are various aspects on which Organisations have to work upon, but the main thing is willingness to accept challenge, change, sacrifice, respect for work, honesty, quality, and giving due respect to individuals who are capable of doing good work.

There has to be a sense of self-satisfaction and desire to excel in whatever one does. Of course, these changes cannot be brought about without a good Leader who has the vision, capability to implement ideas and guide in the right direction. The storm of globalisation is gathering speed and only World Class Organisations will be able to survive and flourish.

INCOMPETENT BOSS

It is believed that those who are competent go higher up on Organisation ladder and many employees are fortunate to have such competent Bosses. But same is not the case with all the employees in some of the Organisations. It is true that performance is the driving factor for climbing the hierarchical ladder, but everyone is not judged in the same manner and the decision makers may have certain parameters which may not be directly related to performance only at workplace.

Some people may occupy seats just because they are related to someone within or outside the Organisation while as someone else may reach to a particular position just because he is able to take care of someone who influences the decision-making process. Like that there can be some more reasons also for such development, which cannot be explained from the point of view of morale, ethics, logic, justice, capability, competence, etc., but are well understood by the people around and by the people who directly get affected. Unfortunately such a thing does happen in some of the Organisation, Professional or Non-Professional, and gets repeated. Certain people take care of doing it very carefully while as others do not bother about anything and practice it openly.

The actions of some of the individuals are influenced more by their own needs, perceptions and personal goals, rather than the needs of the Organisation. Some people cannot control themselves while as some others do not feel need to control. Some see nothing wrong in whatever they do while as some do not want to understand the impact of their actions. What is more important for such individuals is that what they are going to get, rather than the Organisation. Such people think that along with their growth, the Organisation will also grow. Such people think that the Organisation should sacrifice, rather than they sacrificing for the Organisation. Inefficiency in certain pockets does not mean anything to them. They run a race of greed, ego, personal wealth and other external satisfactions rather than a sense of pride in doing useful work.

For all such people results mean only one thing and that is who can help them to achieve their own personal goals, wealth, enjoyment. In turn they take care of all such people who support them for achieving these personal goals and keep their eyes closed towards all the misdeeds. As those who are incompetent, can come up only by such acts, they keep on looking for all such opportunities which can help them in retaining their seats or push them up, even at the cost of the Organisation.

It is also true that some people may be very competent in their work but they cannot resist temptations, temporary short time gains, and hence end up in supporting some incompetent people who provide helping hand to them for such activities. Such competent people may get away with some of their undesirable acts due to Organisation Lethargy and fear in minds of others to get punished or suffer in life if they open their mouth. In any case some people do suffer but those people do not get support from others and hence have to suffer silently. Even if they shout, no one may be there to take action and hence few individuals keep on taking advantage of the situation. When the Top People try to take undue advantage, then inefficient and corrupt people can be seen around who cannot be touched. Such cluster of people can be negligible or may be a large number. It depends upon the history of the Organisation, its age, present and past Culture, Organisation health, its future plans and the way it conducts its business in market. If there is dirt, flies are going to be there. It is the job of Top Management to keep an open eye and prevent misuse of power, but if the Top Management itself is involved in abuse of power, then who can save the Organisation from such people?

Juniors have their own limitations and only in the extreme cases they can muster enough support as well as courage to correct the situation. Normally the abuse of authority is directly related to the way Organisation operates at various levels in various departments, and upon the operating checks or controls. Some people at different levels may try and take chances and see if they can get away with unwanted actions and if they succeed, the Organisation suffers. It depends upon the extent to which the abuse is and also upon the level at which it is being done. It also depends upon the opportunities in different areas and the system of traceability. But if the Culture of the Organisation is straightforward and honest working, then such activities will find difficult to flourish and people will think twice before doing anything wrong or supporting any wrong person. But if the people perceive that the sermons are only for them and not for all, then some will definitely get courage and do what is not desirable. They may even do it openly, justifying their action by giving examples of others. That will set in a Culture where people close their eyes, turn deaf ears for all such activities and messages, resulting in growth of incompetent people day by day.

It is said that if you have poverty, you can distribute poverty only. It all depends upon what has been accumulated and in what proportion. People will do what they see others doing and they will mostly follow the path of least resistance. If the Organisation resists bad habits, bad Culture, then people will avoid those things. Although it is difficult to maintain certain good standards at all levels and by all people, but it is essential and is the need of any Organisation — be at house or market or establishment, or in public life. One does not have any morale ground to stop others from practicing something which he himself is doing and hence, all value systems shall start from Top, others will fall in line. It is true that human beings are different and do not think in the same manner and they are prone to making mistakes, but that is where the systems, controls and those who are in power come into picture.

People in position should do right things and prevent or restrict wrong activities. They are not there to take care of themselves and for keeping their eyes closed. They are not there to support incompetent and greedy people. It is necessary to see what a person is doing himself instead of only seeing what others are doing. It shall be noted that by nature, generally a person would like to do something which gives him satisfaction, peace and prestige. Most of the people do not like to be seen as accused and someone raising finger towards them. Also, people do fear bad advertisement and try to avoid it. There are always exceptions and some people do have tendency to take advantage of the situation and take risk to see if they can get away. Hence, as long as the people are trying to do honest job, they will succeed and can develop very good surrounding with everyone feeling happy. Need is there for self restrain and control, self-respect and sense of pride in whatever one does. There should not be any place for incompetency. The Organisation Culture automatically will improve and good people will flourish.

The biggest punishment for a competent person can be to ask him to work under less competent or incompetent person who comes in the way due to his position and style. Such incompetent Boss may remain happy by hardly doing anything useful and take all the possible advantages, but as finally someone has to answer for the work, the competent person gets affected. The tendency of incompetent Boss can be to support some inefficient people due to other factors and that becomes a reason for irritation as well as roadblock for good people. In any case such incompetent people do not generate any respect for themselves but due to them the other group members also get affected. The competent person will burn himself under such circumstances and still the desired results may not be achieved for which he may be blamed. For competent people, the results are important and they work hard for the same. But their efforts partly get nullified due to presence of incompetent people, especially the Boss. It is better not to have a person like him above rather than having him. Some people can cause more damage to the setup due to their presence. The damage done by their inactivity or bad activities can be much more.

How long and how much other members can repair and recover the lost grounds? It may be difficult and it tells on the group. The image of such groups gets affected and people lose their face due to incompetency of someone, who is not their choice. Hence, it is important to see that such imbalances do not exist and are not supported in the Organisation. In the interest of the

Organisation, the powers of such incompetent person shall be reduced or such person shall be removed. Even if there is some compulsion to keep such incompetent person, it is better to keep him in non-executive post and give him a job which does not affect working of others. Of course, again it depends upon the Authorities who are supporting or promoting and keeping such person in the Organisation and their purpose. Probably that is where others should come in picture and do not keep their eyes and ears closed but do something to remove their own burden and help the Organisation to become better. If people accept to suffer silently and allow unwanted activities, then they should be prepared to get adversely affected also. Hence, it is their responsibility to restrict activities of such people. However, in practice, it is the people at Top who have to be more vigilant, honest and fair in their actions, then only the ill effects of inefficiency can be avoided and groups can function with enthusiasm, higher productivity, sense of belongingness and satisfaction.

SUPER BOSS

Super Boss can be male or female. The article is not to be taken against any particular gender, but the purpose is to highlight certain undesirable practices.

There is one Management Style which is popular in some of the Organisations is Management by Super Boss, i.e. wife of the Boss. This style of Management is practiced in many ways directly or indirectly. First the Boss himself is controlled by his wife and his performance depends upon her mood and orders. If one finds him very happy or too irritated, the reason can be traced to something very good or very bad at home. That day the office atmosphere may be very light or very tense. The chain reaction in office will affect everybody positively or negatively.

The poor Boss may not be able to think of office and may be actually loaded with the house problems and demands. At times these can be very heavy and although he may be present physically in the office, but mentally he may be fully busy on something not at all connected with the office work. He has to cope with the ambitions and high expectations of the Super Boss and her so called status among the other ladies, neighbours, relatives, etc. The Boss is indirectly forced to compete with those who have nothing to do with the office directly. On top of that outside the office the Super Boss expects that the Boss has to look smart and attractive like someone else who charms in parties. He should always be ready to receive, entertain and do whatever is required for each and everyone from the in-law's side, (the preferred relatives of the Super Boss), forgetting all about office ethics as well as rules and regulations.

Now with so many problems from home, how can one remain unaffected? But that's not enough as far as Management Styles are concerned. In some cases, the Super Boss comes to office of the Boss and directs some of the office staff in carrying out their duties. She may have interests in interior decoration, painting, music, drama, social work, games, club activities, gardening, etc., and can suggest number of things for the office and other areas. Naturally her orders will get more importance than the office related orders of the Boss and hence will have to be carried out seriously, and with a sense of urgency. Whether it is part of the Organisation's business or not, it has to be twisted and molded to look as if it is necessary for the business of the Organisation. If the lady gets unhappy on something, then someone or the other has to pay for it heavily. It is to be assumed that she is expert in everything. It is to be remembered all the time that she is a superhuman and that is the reason she is able to control the Boss also.

One has to remember that what belongs to the Organisation should also be available for the use of the great lady, as and when required by her—whether it is Organisation's property, equipment, services, etc., or the manpower. Her travel has to be planned and all the tickets, passes, concessions, must be passed on as per her wishes to various people. Any inconvenience, delay or non-availability of required facilities is going to create problem. If a party hosted by her anywhere for any reason is not arranged efficiently, then the concerned person should be prepared to get the punishment as found fit by her. Individuals are not there for questioning her actions, but are there to follow the orders. How to account the expenses and from where to get the money is not her problem. It is assumed that if one cannot manage even such a small matter and arrange for payments, then he is an inefficient person and hence cannot be a desirable person for the Organisation. As long as one keeps on providing what she wants and takes care of her wishes, his out of turn promotions and grant of other benefits are assured. Unofficially whatever is grabbed by such individuals cannot be objected by anybody. Such people become the trusted people and hence continue in the job directly or indirectly. If there is any time limit it will be applicable only for others. As long as the Super Boss remains happy, nobody can disturb them, but they can definitely disturb others.

As long as the individual is resourceful, and can take care of various matters of the Super Boss, such as matters related to school admissions, property, house construction, maintenance work, servants, drivers, legal and illegal cases, customs clearance, income-tax, passport, police, etc, he can be assured of handsome rewards till the time he becomes physically unfit to do anything. He does not have to worry about his office duties. And when in the office, he can behave most arrogantly with whomsoever he likes, no one will be able to complain against him, as there will be no one to listen or act. If a complaint is made, the person who made the complaint will be made to suffer for daring such a thing against the most sought-after person by Super Boss.

In this type of Organisations, certain people take all the possible advantages and become power brokers. Such people can easily spoil any one's image, whosoever he may be. The people who provide such specialised services to the great lady have to be dealt with carefully, if one wants to keep away from their nuisance. They are like a typical peon of a corrupt official, as they can reach the Super Boss at any time anywhere and whisper in the ears of the great lady anything against any good, efficient and respectable person. Such people acquire dangerous powers without holding any responsible position and use the same with vengeance and meanness. They do not have capacity to do good job in the office but they possess capacity to please certain quarters and take maximum possible advantage out of it. No honest person can work with them and it can be a great punishment for any straightforward executive to have such a person as one of the department employees under his control or as a senior person. Such people by habit appear quite helpful but they actually can bite anytime. Presence of such people can only spoil the department and its name which is immaterial to them as their survival does not depend upon the Departmental Head but depends upon the Super Boss. Such people, if given authority, will play dirty games. As they keep on providing certain specific services to certain specific people and get indulged in certain unauthorised activities, they also get used to receiving special services and unauthorised money. They develop a pool of scrupulous contractors, suppliers and such other people, who try to make money by unfair means.

Of course, there exists other type of Management which remains completely away from all such evils and provide a clean atmosphere at workplace as well as in the society. In such a Management, work is worshiped and there is no place for such scrupulous people. It's a matter of pleasure to work in such surroundings where one can give his best to the Organisation. It is the duty of Top Management to develop a Professional Culture and not to support activities of inefficient and dishonest people. If they can avoid taking certain benefits through such people and practice what they teach to others, then no cunning employee will find a place for himself and will not be able to trouble anybody else. It will also ensure corruption free environment and a healthy, growing Organisation. People will love to work in such an Organisation.

It's to be remembered that the Management is made of people and they decide what type of management practices are to be followed in the place of work or anywhere outside. It's because of them the Organisation gets good image or bad image. In any good Organisation, there should not be any place for any Super Boss or such people who work against the interest of the establishment. Every Boss must keep all such unwanted people away and develop good atmosphere at workplace so that people enjoy their work and contribute positively for the growth of the Organisation.

ORGANISATION ENERGY

An Organisation is made of people. The combined energy of these people keeps the life of Organisation ticking. The health of all the organs of the Organisation depends upon how healthy the employees are and how much energy they utilise or waste during the course of their work. Sickness of some organs can affect the whole body slowly and one day it may become severe, if not detected and attended in time. If the problem is like cancerous cell, then it can keep on spreading, if not cured, and one day grow to such an extent that no medicine may work. In order to avoid such a situation, it is necessary to remain vigilant, carry out Organisation's health checkup regularly and attend problem areas well in time. Detection should lead to remedial steps and preventive measures to avoid recurrence of the symptoms.

An Organisation can become weak due to loss of energy on various counts which results in reduced capacity to fight and become susceptible to outside attacks. The loss of energy can be in different forms but basically it is due to the people and also because of systems and procedures which are manmade, which can be corrected. However sometimes a change may become very difficult due to the amount of work involved and hence timely action at regular intervals is necessary.

As far as people are concerned, their behaviour partly depends upon Organisation's Culture. If it is healthy, unwanted behaviour will not be able to flourish easily and hence there will be less loss of energy of people. However, it gets affected by personal ego, ambitions, prejudices, fixations, education, upbringing, etc. In case of personality clashes, personal egos are involved which encourages infighting and the main goal of working to improve health of Organisation gets sidetracked. These leakages of energy occur regularly in many departments and at various levels. In the process job requirements get second priority, the work does not get attended as required and within the time it is to be carried out.

Incompetency is also another source of loss of energy. Each incompetent person affects efficiency of many other people. The extent of effect depends upon the degree of incompetency and the position person is holding. If the Organisation cannot separate out weeds, then one day there will be weeds all over and it may become difficult to do anything.

There has to be inbuilt system to identify the source of loss of energy and a system to plug the loopholes. Organisation should have courage and should be willing to take remedial measures, otherwise failure of organs will occur silently and there may not be any remedy possible afterwards or it may be very difficult and time consuming.

Money is another factor for loss of energy and it can cripple the Organisation. Money not spent properly, not utilised effectively, or pilfered, can reduce the oxygen level of the Organisation and sometimes not allow it to even stand on its feet. People in the Organisation can do nothing without money and its judicious use as well as availability is extremely important for the Organisation to continue operating. Organisations having enough money can also suffer if the funds are not invested properly. Equipments, machineries, material and other resources, also require proper attention. Like over eating or under eating affects the functioning of body, similarly all the facilities are required in proper proportion and have to be utilised effectively. All these actions depend upon the competency of people involved and hence what really counts is how efficient and sincere are the employees in the Organisation.

Although everyone in the Organisation is important, but some count more than others. The Leaders can take other people in right or wrong direction. The Leaders can create an environment of healthy or unhealthy working atmosphere. All the cells and parts of the body are important and have specific function to perform, but it's the Brain which directs and controls their functioning and the cells work as per the state of mind. Hence employing and placement of effective Leaders is very important for efficient working and progress of the Organisation and to avoid its loss of energy.

If all the available energy is directed and utilised in right direction without losses, the Organisation can do wonders and no one will be able to slow down its progress and prosperity. Then the Organisation can grow very well and all the people involved can share the fruits of their good work.

THE MANAGEMENT STYLES

There are different types of Management Styles prevailing in the World, however they may fall in three main categories – Non-Professional, Professional and Governmental type of Management. Each one has its own typical Style of Management. The most talked about and praised is Professional type of Management, which is considered more successful and desirable. In this type of Management, Team Performance is generally given more importance.

Non-Professional type depends more upon one or very few individuals and some of them remain quite secretive including their Business Practices. Governmental type face interference from politicians and government officials, in different proportion at different places, and some of them end up with poor performance due to absence of required accountability, although some still manage to do a good job.

It is generally understood that Professional Managements employ people on their merits and equal opportunity is provided to everyone to prove himself and reach to higher positions. Nonperformers are not expected to retain their positions in such Organisations and no favouritism is expected. In this type of Management there is more talk of moral, ethics, etc, in public life and of their own Organisation values. People from these Organisations sometimes criticise government machinery and politicians for corruption, lethargy, favouritism, etc. Some of them blame the Government for slow growth and delays. People give examples of professionalism and high productivity levels in other Countries and wish that the same system, procedures are adopted in their own Country also.

However, it is also true that some of the professionals who talk about ethics, good Corporate Governance, etc., themselves do not follow high standards. In reality, nonprofessional things do happen behind the curtains, which get covered under the mask of Professional Organisation.

In order to have better understanding of the Management Styles, it may be worthwhile to go through some of the "Behind the Curtain Activities" which may be in practice in some of the Organisations or followed by some professionals. Some of these activities may be more prevalent in Upcoming or Less Developed Countries, but it all depends on people in position working in any Organisation, anywhere in the World. ENRON failed in 2001 in one of the most Developed Country, USA, and SATYAM failed in 2009 in one of the fastest Developing Country, INDIA, both because of the failure of Top Management and absence of required Checks and Controls, etc. There are similar examples in some other Countries also. It will be worthwhile to understand what all happened in such Organisations, which resulted in their collapse. However other than larger Frauds, some undesirable activities at operating level do affect the Organisations.

In some cases, various decisions starting from recruitment, promotions, etc., to setting up new Unit or facility may get influenced by factors other than merit also. Decision process of some professionals may remain different than entrepreneurs due to personal factors. Instead of choosing most profitable business locations suitable for new Units, additional capacities, etc., some people may tend to give preference to their own state of origin, possibility of personal growth and comfort level. As Professional Organisation generally have senior people from different parts of the Country, sometimes tussle may start in such matters and it depends upon who is more powerful, the decision may go in his favour. Suitable project reports then may become more of a formality.

In large Professional Organisations, recruitment is carried out mostly on country level or even from other Countries, depending upon specific requirements and availability of people. A proper mix is generally expected and it is believed that no favors are done in the selection process. However careful examination of such recruitment may indicate that in some cases, some specific group of candidates got preference for reasons best known to selectors. In due course of time that group may occupy key positions and generally may remain dominant in the Organisation. Of course, the professional touch also ensures that some other good people also get recruited and they also come up, but it may be difficult for such people to enter in the core group of Top Management, barring few exceptions, which can be due to some extraordinary capabilities or some connections.

When it comes to promotions in such set ups, it becomes comparatively easy for specific group of people to come up as they may get support from all levels due to majority factor and also due to building up of proper background throughout the year or over a long period of time in order to look as justified decisions. In any case they may end up getting all good assignments and in some cases their failures, if any, may be taken care of properly. The minority group or impartial people having no specific group, may have to work hard and some of the capable people may face problems, resistance, and there may be attempt to put them down also, which outwardly may look justified. Although these people may be very efficient but may find it difficult to fight back due to lack of necessary support which majority group gets automatically most of the time. And thus, the building up of group strength continues at various levels.

In some Countries, especially Developing Countries, it can be checked that in number of cases the next person coming up in the Department or Organisation at higher levels may belong to a specific group which can be traced to the Department Head or Organisation Head, barring some exceptions which may be due to non-availability of required experienced person, or due to extraordinary capabilities of an individual. There will be also many examples of impartial decisions in such matters and for that credit must go to the people in position.

In some cases, particular person or few specific people may occupy key positions even at the cost of Organisation due to certain other reasons. Their inefficiency may negatively affect the Organisation but it may get justified as long as those people are "Senior's Men". Less profit or losses of that group may get side tracked. People may not dare to question it openly.

The Zamindari system has almost gone, the old system of Rulers has disappeared in Democracies, but there is a new set of Zamindars and Rulers who have come up and are occupying positions in various Organisations, be it Professional or Non-Professional or Government Organisation. In some cases, it is well known and the show goes on while as in some other cases it is not well known and is not expected also in those Organisations. These new Zamindars or Rulers remain busy in increasing their own influence, or may go on amassing wealth for themselves and in the process may have negative effect on the Organisation in the long run. Their powers need to be curtailed at right time.

It may also happen that even for selecting top most person, highly talented, knowledge or research-based Organisation may get divided on the lines of specific group, although it should not happen in such Organisations. One can imagine how the evil of cast or creed or regionalism, etc, can influence the working place and life in general. One can find such examples in various fields including politics. In some Countries, even nation's top most positions get affected with some other considerations instead of capabilities only, so how they can expect to get best out of the people and compete on equal footings with other more efficient nations? Hence Organisations have to take corrective steps in controlling undesirable activities which may be going on behind the curtains in their own set up also.

The vision of an individual Organisation may not get fulfilled due to some of the unwanted practices which may come in the way of creativity, good individual performance, honest working and maintaining certain ethics. As the Government Organisations are observed and politicians are watched regularly, one comes to know more often about what wrong is being done by them, but functioning of other Organisations is not watched in a similar manner and limited information remains available to public in general. Thus, some of their undesirable deeds remain mostly hidden.

More the things remain hidden, more will be negative impact which will continue and increase in proportion. Hence every Organisation should take out the dirt, and move forward to achieve real progress as required in order to compete efficiently. It is not a matter of type of Management only, but it is a matter of style of functioning of people in position also and their intensions. Very few Organisations may be able to claim that everything is ok in all the departments and at all levels. Hence suitable steps are required to be taken in most of the Organisations, the extent of such action may vary considerably depending upon the existing status and it has to be an ongoing process.

TEAM WORKERS V/S LEADERS

Every Organisation and Group needs a Leader to lead it in a particular direction and every Leader needs Team Workers to carry out the work successfully. Both are needed and both are made for each other. Each one has its own place and the Society or Organisation cannot function effectively in absence of any one of them. Although there may be number of people acting as Leaders but those who can really fulfill the requirements of a real Leader are few. Society is actually feeling shortage of good Leaders.

It is also necessary to understand the effect of Team

Workers and Leaders on each other and see if Leaders are functioning as Leaders or getting converted to Team Workers and whether Leaders are vanishing due to Team Work Culture. Team Workers can continue to do good work as long as there is a Leader somewhere taking care of all leadership related issues or problems, like a child in the vicinity of his mother. The Team Workers survive on the pillars made of the Leaders. If a Leader goes away, the Team performance may get adversely affected within a short period because the Team may become directionless and uncontrollable. The fact is that Teams require a Leader and Team Workers require directives. Teams can support an engine but they may not be able to replace an engine. Teams require starters and require regulators. The Leader possesses necessary vision to direct the Team in right direction.

Without a Leader, the Teams are like body without soul. Team Workers are good people who can work in harmony with others but they cannot make history. They can understand and transform thoughts of Leader into action, give suggestions, and follow decisions. Teams can work on a smoother known road or can work on rough terrain if someone keeps on directing. The Leader may be part of the Team or he may be outside the Team but the fact is that a Leader is required and it is his foresight, which really takes everyone in a particular direction.

It is also a fact that without Teams and their good work, a Leader cannot achieve results and can be a paper tiger only. But the Teams without proper goal and mission can be like a boat in the mid sea and can get lost completely. Leaders are always individuals having required energy levels and force to move along and take people with them or make them to follow. Teams are made of the people who follow the Leader to achieve a mission. No one can survive without the other but Teams can be made from many people, while as Leaders may be in short supply. Teams can be changed, new members can be added, but Leaders cannot be brought in with same ease.

Leaders have capacity to take decisions, give direction and achieve goals. Degree of success or failure may depend upon many factors including environment and the size of the task, but what is certain is that the Leaders will bring in change — liked or not liked by people. There may be resistance as people cannot foresee what Leader can, and hence the Leader has to work hard with firmness depending upon the severity of the situation. It is the capacity of the Leader to take right decision at right time which makes him different from others. It is the capacity of the Leader to take tough and sometimes unpopular decisions, which makes him different. Those who are power hungry cannot be termed as good Leaders, as their purpose is not to serve people or Organisation effectively but to enjoy the fruits of power.

There are Good Leaders and Bad Leaders. A Dacoit is also a Leader who is able to gather a Team of people for carrying out dacoity. That is also one type of Team Work and is dangerous also. No one should support such Leaders, they are Negative Leaders. Similarly the people who try to push the mankind to destruction should also not get any support. Humanity needs Positive Leaders. Humanity needs Mahaveer, Buddha, Jesus, and Mohammed. Humanity needs people like Gandhiji, who are selfless and who are interested in working for masses, or for their Teams, Organisations. Welfare of the Team members has to be part of their goal. They should not use the people but should care for them.

A good Leader can maintain Teamwork and get results from Team members provided he is working honestly for the goal and is able to support the Team in case of any difficulty. The Leaders do not run away but face the situation and try to find out solutions. They are tuned to find out a way. The Team Members may or may not go through the full life of the mission, but the Leader accomplishes it. He is there throughout in thick and thin of it. He is there in the forefront. Those who push the Team Member in front and remain behind to save themselves cannot be called Leaders.

In some cases, Teamwork is given much more importance than it deserves, which affects the performance of the Leader. In such a situation, Team Members who are not capable may end up getting undue importance and get heard at the cost of the task and mission. The Team Leader may end up in making certain adjustments at the cost of the task and results. The blame goes to the Leader for not achieving the results but actually he is restricted sometimes from moving ahead due to imposed factor of keeping all the Team Members happy.

Organisation should be people sensitive but not at the cost of the task. Failures cannot be accepted as other good Team Members get demoralised. A group of such Teams having poor performance and less bothered about the results cannot generate a good fertile ground for Leaders to come up and actually works as a slow poison for them. Such atmosphere cannot bring up a tall Leader but can throw him away and allow only small shortsighted Leaders who cannot take the Organisation to higher heights.

Human feelings are important but everyone has to understand that they are not there to run a dying Organisation. The Organisation should not collapse due to its own weight. Some amount of corrective action is necessary and, in the process, few people will be always unhappy. If the environment allows such steps then the Organisation can grow and the Leader can take it to greater heights.

The Organisation Culture should support good cause and allow a Leader to complete the task. Supporting a Good Leader is responsibility of the society or employees and it is in their own interest. It is important to not only recognise the Leader, but should also not allow some groups of people to pull him down. Everyone has to work enthusiastically to achieve the goal. After discussions, Leader's decisions shall be accepted so that the task can be accomplished and everyone can enjoy the fruits of his vision and capacity.

SELECTION FOR TOP POSITIONS

As Industrial, Financial and Digital activities are going on increasing all over the world, more and more New Business Ventures are coming up regularly. It has resulted in increased demand for suitable experienced senior management personnel who can handle responsibility independently and have proper understanding of the business process. Different set ups will have different requirements for the task to be accomplished and hence it is important that enough care is taken in filling up such vacancies as it can have positive or negative impact in the long run. Apart from the sixth sense of the Selector, it would be better to keep in mind the requirement of some of the following traits of a person (as applicable for specific position) while going through the selection process of candidates for top positions :-

1. Is he able to work independently and take sound decisions for future in reasonable time?
2. Does he possess the ability to quickly analyse problems, understand the intricacies involved and timely implement suitable action?
3. Is he creative and can he implement new ideas successfully?
4. Is he resourceful and can he gather necessary support from various quarters when required?
5. Is he fair in his dealings and will he give necessary freedom to work, depending upon the capabilities of individuals?
6. Is he honest and whether the Organisation's interests will remain safe in his hands?
7. Can he be firm and take hard decisions if the situation demands

and is he prepared to face difficulties?
8. Can he represent the Organisation effectively and deal at various levels outside the Organisation?
9. Can he understand various functions of the Organisation quickly and concentrate on the main points?
10. Is he capable of taking risk and can he lead the Teams to success?
11. Can he build the Organisation from scratch or he can only maintain it after someone else has built it?
12. Is he a self-starter, sufficiently motivated and has enough drive?
13. Is he technically competent in his own field and can he appreciate new technology?
14. Is he versatile and can he co-ordinate with various groups and agencies effectively?
15. Is he willing to change with the demands of different situations and take advantage of latest developments?

16. Does he possess good communication and presentation skills?
17. Is he open-minded, willing to listen to others point of view, learn from mistakes and move forward?
18. Is he going to lead the team "From Front" and will he be willing to take responsibility for failures?
19. Is he impartial and will he provide equal opportunity to all deserving people?
20. Will he respect competent executives and develop healthy working atmosphere? At the same time can he be tough with poor performers?
21. Does he possess clear vision? Can he set high standards and make the Organisation one of the best in the field, as well as achieve sufficient growth?
22. Can he establish good work ethics and earn good image for the Organisation?
23. Does he understand business intricacies?

24. Can he be diplomatic and attend to problems with cool mind? Is he mature enough to suit the position?
25. In case of a Joint-Venture with Multi-National Organisations, can he understand international business, deal with foreigners effectively and can he look after interests of both the sides?
26. Is he having the ability to select right people and give them necessary support to function without undue interference?
27. Can he withstand pressure from unions, politicians, influential officials, etc., and avoid corruption?
28. Will he continue with the Organisation for a reasonable period of time?
29. Is he having a good track record?

In addition to the above mentioned aspects, if a person is to be given a chance from within the Organisation, then he should NOT be appointed just because -

(i) There is nobody else available immediately.
(ii) He has close relationship with the Appointing Authority.
(iii) He is due for promotion.
(iv) He will remain obedient and will follow the instructions blindly.
(iv) He is well-connected and has been recommended by someone well-placed.
(v) He is good in his present position (may not be able to come up to expectation in the new assignment).

If a person from within the Organisation is found suitable, then he should be given the responsibility only if he is really interested in taking up new assignment wholeheartedly and should be willing to shift to any new location (if required) without pre-conditions. New set up requires a person's "Full Presence", and if the job is given to a partially willing person, the Unit will suffer.

When a person is to be taken from outside then he should not be taken just because he is holding similar position. He might be holding the position due to various reasons and hence, one has to be careful. Also, a candidate should not be rejected on the basis of some feedback which is not verified. However, more care is required if a Top Position Person is being selected for a Green Field Business Venture.

Looking after a well set Organisation is completely different from setting up a new Unit, which requires combination of "Architect", "Builder", and a "Maintenance Man". In a new Organisation, one has to face new situations every day and the person may have to take immediate decisions without help of others and precedents. He has to set up the whole Organisation from scratch, and hence, has to be much more creative, independent thinker, tough, firm, and should be willing to go through hardship.

When an Organisation comes up with some new Units, smaller Units may get less attention, which can affect selection of senior executives also. This may have negative impact on the new Unit. Although difference due to Large and Small size of Business Units cannot be avoided, it should be realised that the process involved in setting up these Units is going to be of similar nature. Smaller Unit may have to go through more problems due to limited finance, facilities and manpower. Selections made keeping in mind these aspects will ensure success and growth of the Organisation.

www.ingramcontent.com/pod-product-compliance
Lightning Source LLC
Chambersburg PA
CBHW070420220526
45466CB00004B/1480